to Steve,

ANIMAL CRACKER UPPERS JR.

RICHARD LEDERER & JIM ERTNER

International Punsters of the Year

ILLUSTRATIONS BY JIM MCLEAN

Marion Street Press

Portland, Oregon

To my daughter Gail and grandson Bryce, my family's
Maine members. —Jim Ertner

To my new grandchildren—
Isaac and Zoe. —Richard Lederer

Published by Marion Street Press
4207 SE Woodstock Blvd # 168
Portland, OR 97206-6267
USA
http://www.marionstreetpress.com/

Orders and review copies: (800) 888-4741

Printed in the United States of America
ISBN 978-1-936863-50-1

Library of Congress Cataloging-in-Publication Data Pending

CONTENTS

INTRODUCTION 5

A (Aardvark-Armadillo) 7
B (Baboon-Butterfly) 11
C (Camel-Crow) 17
D (Dachshund-Duck) 24
E (Eagle-Ewe) 30
F (Fawn-Frog) 33
G (Giraffe-Great Dane) 38
H (Hare-Hyena) 43
I (Iguana-Insect) 48
J (Jackal-Jellyfish) 50
K (Kangaroo-Kitten) 52
L (Lemming-Lobster) 54
M (Mare-Mussel) 57
N (Newt-Nightingale) 61
O (Octopus-Oyster) 62
P (Parrot-Puppy) 65
Q (Quahog-Quail) 71
R (Rabbit-Rooster) 72
S (Salmon-Swordfish) 75
T (Tadpole-Turtle) 82

ANIMAL CRACKER UPPERS JR.

U (Unicorn) 86
V (Vampire–Vulture)..................................87
W (Wallaby–Wren) 89
X (Xiphiidae) 94
Y (Yak) 95
Z (Zebra) 96

INTRODUCTION

Animal jokes
scamper and scramble,
hop and jump,
soar and swoop,
creep and crawl,
burrow and dig,
swim and dive,
and run and gallop
through our lives.

Duck jokes quack us up.

Porcupine jokes are sharp and to-the-point.

Elephant jokes are worth the weight.

Skunk jokes are real stinkers, but they become best-smellers.

Lion jokes are rip-roaring funny.

Zebra jokes are black and white and read all over.

Vampire jokes totally suck, but they have a lot of bite.

Here are more than 500 animal jokes that are guaranteed to make you

    bark,
        bellow,
            bray,
                screech,
                    squawk,
                        squeal,
                            snort,
                                and roar

with lots of laughter.

Aardvark

Aardvark: Aan aanimal that resembles the aanteater.

Alligator

What do you call a creature that has huge jaws and a tail, and lives in dark places between buildings?

An alleygator.

What is an alligator's favorite book?

Swamp Animals *by Al E. Gator and Crockett Dial.*

Animals (in general)

Why can't some animals keep secrets?

Because parrots talk, pigs squeal, yaks yak, and someone always lets the cat out of the bag.

Did you hear about the allergic animals at the zoo?

They broke out.

Why isn't farming an easy life?

You go to sleep with the chickens, get up with the roosters, work like a horse, eat like a pig, and they treat you like a dog and pay you chicken feed.

What did the spelling teacher say to the gorilla?

"U R N N M L."

The Animal Fair

I went to the animal fair.
The birds and the beasts were there.
The big baboon, by the light of the moon,
Was combing his auburn hair.

You should have seen the monk.
He climbed up the elephant's trunk.
The elephant sneezed and fell to his knees,
And that was the end of the monk.

The animal fair, the animal fair,
We had such fun when we were there.
There never was a fair to compare
With that rollicking, frolicking animal fair.

A holiday greeting from the animals: "We Fish Ewe A Furry Meowy Christmas Panda Hippo Gnu Deer."

Ant

Why was the young insect confused?
All his uncles were ants.

What are the largest ants?
A gi-ant and an eleph-ant.

There once was a fellow from France
Whose hobby was searching for ants,
Till he took quite a spill
In a tiny red hill
And wound up with ants in his pants.

A first-time airplane passenger looked out the window and marveled to his companion, "Look at those tiny people down there. They look like ants."

"They are ants," came the reply. "We haven't taken off yet."

Ape

What does a baby gorilla sleep on?
An ape-ri-cot.

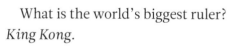

What is the world's biggest ruler?
King Kong.

Why did King Kong climb up the Empire State Building?
He was too big to fit in an elevator.

Did you hear about the big gorilla that invented a bell that would ring whenever a point was won in a table tennis game?

It was called the King Kong Ping Pong Ding Dong.

Armadillo

An armadillo is a possum on the half shell.

Did you hear about the new book titled *Animals With Armor Protection?*

It's by R. Madillo.

Baboon

What kind of apes talk a lot?
Blab-boons.

What do you call a flying monkey?
A hot air baboon.

What kind of monkey is always exploding?
A baBOOM.

Bat

Did you hear about the flying mammal that performed in the circus?

It was an acro-bat.

Why couldn't the vampires field a baseball team?

All their bats flew away.

Beagle

What does Snoopy eat for breakfast?

Beagle and cream cheese.

Did you hear about the dog who joined the Boy Scouts?

He became a beagle scout.

Bear

What do you call a naked grizzly?

A bare bear.

Fuzzy Wuzzy was a bear.
Fuzzy Wuzzy had no hair.
Fuzzy Wuzzy wasn't very fuzzy. Was he?

What did the teddy bear say when he was done eating?

"I'm stuffed!"

Did you hear about the two dumb guys who went to see the bears at Yellowstone National Park?

When they saw a sign that said "Bear left," they went home.

What animal do you look like when you're in the shower?

A little bear.

What do you call a toothless grizzly?
A gummy bear.

Beaver

What did the beaver say to the tree?
"It's been nice gnawing you."

Be like a beaver. Don't get stumped. Just cut things down to size and build for the future.

Bee

What insect gets A's in English class?
A spelling bee.

Why is the letter A like a flower?
Because a B always comes after it.

There was a man who loved the bees.
He always was their friend.
He liked to sit upon their hives,
But they stung him in the end.

Knock, knock.
Who's there?
Zombies.
Zombies who?
Zombies make honey, and zombies don't.

What is black and yellow on the outside and black and yellow on the inside and drives down the street?
A school bus full of bees.

What's worse than being with a fool?
Fooling with a bee.

When does B come after U?
When you take some of its honey.

Bird

What sign did the two birds place above their nest?
"Home Tweet Home."

What do birds say on Halloween?
"Twick or tweet."

Why do birds fly south for the winter?
It's too far to walk.

What do you call a bath in cold water?
A brrrrrd bath.

Why did the bird sign up for Twitter?
So it could tweet.

What birds are always unhappy?
Bluebirds.

Be like the birds. They have bills, too, but they keep on singing.

Bison

What did the buffalo say to his boy when he departed on a long journey?
"Bison."

Boa

Did you hear about the two boa constrictors that got married?

They had a crush on each other.

After the boa constrictor escaped from the zoo, what sign did they put on its empty cage?

"Out to crunch."

What do snakes wear with a tuxedo?

A boa tie.

Boxer

Why did the dog go to the corner whenever the doorbell rang?

It was a Boxer.

Bug

What's the quickest way for a bug to get from the ground to a tree trunk?

Take the shortest root.

Did you hear about the female bedbug?

She had a baby in the spring.

Bulldog

Dad: "Why are you making faces at that bulldog?"

Son: "He started it."

Burro

What do you call a little burro?

A burrito.

Butterfly

A butterfly will flutter by.

Why did the boy throw margarine out of the kitchen window?

He wanted to see butterfly.

Camel

A camel is a horse that swallowed its saddle.

What do soldiers use to hide from their enemies in the desert?

Camelflage.

What do you get when you cross a camel with a cow?
Lumpy milkshakes.

Canary

What did the 500-pound canary say as it walked down the street?
"Here kitty, kitty!"

What do you call a canary run over by a lawnmower?
Shredded tweet.

A woman brought along her pet canary each day that she drove to work.
The little bird was her flying car pet.

Cat

What is the color of a happy cat?
Purrple.

What is the worst weather for mice.
When it's raining cats and dogs.

Did you hear about the cat who was walking along the beach on Christmas Eve?
He had sandy claws.

Where did the kittens go on their class trip?
To a mew-see-'em.

Why is a cat drinking milk like a track star?
Because they both enjoy taking a few laps.

When do cats and dogs get along together?
When you have hot dogs with catsup.

Be like a cat. Claw your way to the top. That's what curtains are for.

Cattle

Where do cows go for entertainment?
To the moovies and to amoosment parks.

What two members of the cow family go everywhere with you?
Your calves.

Knock, knock.
Who's there?
Cattle.
Cattle who?
Cattle always purr when you stroke it.

Where did the cow go when it jumped over the moon?
It went to the Milky Way.

Why do cows have bells around their necks?
Because their horns don't work.

Centipede

Teacher: "Why were you late to school this morning?"
Centipede student: "It took me an hour to put on my galoshes."

What is a centipede's favorite toy?
Leg-os.

A centipede was happy quite, until a frog in fun
Said, "Pray, which leg comes after which?"
This raised her mind to such a pitch,
She lay distracted in a ditch
Considering how to run.

What has a hundred legs and goes, "Ho ho ho!"?
A Santapede.

What did the centipede say to the octopus?
"You're missing 92 feet."

Did you hear about the speedy centipede that won a race by a hundred feet?

What do you get when you cross a chicken with a centipede?
We don't know, but EVERYONE gets a leg.

Chicken

What do you call a hen that gets sunburned in Florida?
Southern fried chicken.

What games do ghost chickens play?
Peck-a-boo and peep-a-boo.

Why couldn't the hen find her eggs?
Because she mislaid them.

What did one little chicken say to another when it found a fruit in their nest?
"Look at the orange Mama laid."

What do baby chickens like to read?
Peeple Magazine.

What noise does Rice Chickies cereal make?
"Snap, cackle, and peep."

Chimpanzee

What is a chimp's favorite energy candy?
Monkey bars.

What is a monkey's favorite dessert?
Chocolate chimp cookies.

What did the chimpanzee say when his sister had a baby?
"Well, I'll be a monkey's uncle."

Cockatoo

What is a cockatoo called after it's two years old?
A cockathree.

Cockroach

Did you hear about the cockroach doll?
You wind it up and it runs under the kitchen sink.

Collie

What are dog biscuits made from?
Collie flour.

Crab

How much does a crab eat?
Just a pinch.

What sea animal gives people rides?
A taxi crab.

Crane

What bird can lift the most weight?
A crane.

Crocodile

You will find by the banks of the Nile
The place of the great crocodile.
He will welcome you in
With an innocent grin,
Which gives way to a satisfied smile.

While on a safari in Africa, a man decided to take a refreshing swim in a river. He asked the guide if there were any sharks in the water and was told there weren't any.

After diving in, the man shouted to the guide, "Are you sure there are no sharks in here?"

"No sharks," came the reply. "Sharks are afraid of crocodiles."

Crow

What is a ghost's favorite kind of bird?

> *A scare crow.*

Did you hear about the scarecrow?

> *It was so scary that the crows not only stopped stealing corn, but they also brought back the corn they stole last year.*

Why is a royal blackbird like a frog?

> *Because it's crow king.*

Sign in pet store: "Caw us and we'll tweet you right."

Dachshund

A dachshund is half a dog high by a dog-and-a-half long.

What is taller sitting down than standing up?
> *A dachshund.*

Why is the dachshund a good family dog?
> *Because all the members of the family can pet it at the same time.*

Dalmatian

Why do Dalmatians have a hard time hiding?
Because they're always spotted.

What's black and white and black and white and black
and white and black and white and black and white and
black and white and black and white and black and white
and black and white and black and white and black and
white and black and white and black and white and black
and white and black and white and black and white and
black and white and black and white and black and white
and black and white and black and white and black and
white and black and white and black and white and black
and white and black and white and black and white and
black and white and black and white and black and white
and black and white and black and white and black and
white and black and white and black and white and black
and white and black and white and black and white and
black and white and black and white and black and white
and black and white and black and white and black and
white and black and white and black and white and black
and white and black and white and black and white and
black and white and black and white and black and white
and black and white and black and white and black and
white and black and white and black and white and black
and white and black and\ white and black and white and
black and white and black and white and black and white
and black and white and black and white and black and
white and black and white and black and white and black
and white and black and white and black and white and
black and\ white and black and white and black and white
and black and white and black and white and black and
white and black and white and black and white and black

and white and black and white?

The answer is 101 Dalmatians.

Deer

Why are does so fast?

> *Because they sometimes have to run for their deer lives.*

What do you get when you cross a deer and a ghost?

> *Bamboo.*

Dinosaur

A dinosaur is a colossal fossil.

> *There once was a Tyrannosaurus*
> *That lived when the earth was all porous.*
> *But it fainted with shame*
> *When it first heard its name,*
> *And departed the earth long before us.*

What do you get when dinosaurs crash their cars?

> *Tyrannosaurus wrecks.*

Why don't they include dinosaurs in animal crackers?

> *Because they'd be too big to fit in the box.*

What dinosaur roamed the Wild West?

> *Tyrannosaurus Tex, riding his Bronco-saurus.*

Dog

Did you hear about the baseball dog?

> *He chases fowls, catches flies, loves to walk, and runs for home when he sees the catcher coming.*

> *There was a young man from St. Paul*
> *Who attended a fancy dress ball.*
> *He said he would risk it*
> *And went as a biscuit,*
> *But a dog bit his leg in the hall.*

Why did the dog have to appear in court?

> *Because it got a barking ticket.*

What's the opposite of a cool cat?

> *A hot dog.*

What do you call a cold canine?

> *A chili dog.*

Why does a dog get so hot in the summer?

> *Because he wears a coat and pants.*

Be like a dog. Be loyal. Enjoy the wind in your face. Run barefoot, romp, and play daily. Leave yourself breathless at least once a day. And leave your mark on the world.

Donkey

What keys won't open doors?

> *Donkeys (as well as monkeys and turkeys).*

Dragon

How do dragons vent their frustrations?
They let off steam.

Why do dragons sleep during the day?
So they can hunt knights.

Why don't baby dragons like to eat knights?
They hate canned food.

Duck

As an intro-duck-tion, did you hear about the farmer who named his pet duck Hickory Dickory?

What is a duck's favorite snack?
Cheese and quackers.

Why was the duck so smart?
Because it always made wise quacks.

A girl duck went to the store to buy some lipstick and told the saleslady, "Put it on my bill."

What has webbed feet and fangs?
Count Quackula.

What is a duck's favorite ballet?
"The Nutquacker."

What bird is useful in boxing matches?
  Duck.

Be like a duck. Keep calm and unruffled on the surface of the water, but paddle like crazy underneath.

Eagle

Illegal: A sick bird.

What bird never goes to a barber?
    A bald eagle.

Why do eagles go to church?
    Because they're birds of pray.

Be like an eagle. Travel in the highest circles, stay eagle-eyed, and swoop down on every opportunity.

Eel

What is an eel's favorite sport?
Ice shockey.

Did you hear the story about the slippery eel?
Never mind. You wouldn't be able to grasp it.

Where do young fish study and learn?
In eel-ementary schools.

> *A speedy young swimmer named Block*
> *Was the fastest away from the dock.*
> *He broke records galore*
> *Till they found that he wore*
> *An electric eel stuffed in his jock.*

Elephant

Why did the baby elephant put its teeth under its pillow?
For the tusk fairy.

How do you make an elephant fly?
First, you get a huge zipper . . . .

What do you give a seasick elephant?
Plenty of room.

Who weighs 6,000 pounds and wears glass slippers?
Cinderelephant.

Why aren't elephants allowed on some beaches?
Because they can't keep their trunks up.

How can you tell if there is an elephant in your refrigerator?

Look for his footprint in the Jell-O.

How many giraffes will fit in the refrigerator?

None. There's already an elephant in there.

What would you get if Batman and Robin were trampled by a herd of elephants?

Flatman and Ribbon.

Ewe

What is a sheep's favorite website?

EweTube.

Why did the ram run over the cliff?

He didn't see the ewe turn.

Fawn

What did the buck say to the doe?
"Let's have a little fawn, baby."

Firefly

Did you hear about the two fireflies that met at sunrise?
It was love at first light.

As the boy firefly said to his girlfriend, "I really glow for you."

How do firefly races begin?

The referee shouts, "Ready, set, glow!"

What did the frog have for a light meal?

A firefly.

What did the mother firefly say to her husband while looking at their son?

"He's bright for his age, isn't he?"

Fish

Fish sleep in river beds, wash themselves in river basins, keep their money in river banks, and roe, roe, roe their river boats. Here are some finny fishy lines:

What did one bass say to another?

"Keep your big mouth shut, and you won't get caught!"

What did the Cinderella fish wear to the ball?

Glass flippers.

How do you communicate with a fish?

By dropping it a line.

Sign at a seafood market: "Our fish come from the best schools."

Sign at another fish market: "If our fish were any fresher, they'd be insulting."

Flamingo

Why do flamingos stand on one leg?

Because if they picked up the other leg, they'd fall over.

Be like a flamingo. Don't be afraid to look odd as long as you have a leg to stand on.

Flea

What do you get when you cross a flea with a rabbit?

A bugs bunny.

How do you start a flea race?

By shouting, "One, two, flea, go!"

How do fleas travel?

They itch-hike.

> *A flea and a fly in a flue*
> *Were imprisoned, so what could they do?*
> *Said the flea, "Let us fly!"*
> *Said the fly, "Let us flee!"*
> *So they flew through a flaw in the flue.*

Did you hear about the dog who went to a flea circus?

He stole the show.

As one flea said to another, "Shall we walk or take the dog?"

> *Some say that fleas are black,*
> *But I know that's not so,*
> *'Cause Mary had a little lamb*
> *With fleas as white as snow.*

Flounder

A man with a bad disease was put in a hospital room. A doctor was called in and told the man, "We're going to feed you all the flounder, pancakes, and pizza you can eat."

"That's great!" said the man. "Will this cure me?"

"Cure you?" replied the doctor. "No! That's all we can slide under the door."

Fly

Have you ever seen a horse fly?

What kind of paper is best for making kites?
>*Flypaper.*

Nothing makes one hotter
Than wielding a fly swatter.
But it's all we've got
To teach those flies what's swat.

A mother fly complained after a sleepless night, "Junior was sick, and I had to walk the ceiling with him all night."

The hand is quicker than the eye is,
But somewhat slower than the fly is.

What did the fly say to the flypaper?
>*"I'm stuck on you."*

What has four wheels and flies?
>*A garbage truck.*

Why will the computer never replace the newspaper?
>*You can't swat flies and line the bottom of a birdcage with a computer.*

Frog

What do you call a frog with a cast on each of its back legs?

Unhoppy.

What is the name of the new science fantasy film epic in which the main characters are frogs?

Star Warts.

What is a frog's favorite kind of music?

Hip hop.

What is a frog's favorite snack?

French flies and a large Croak at the IHOP.

What was the frog's job at the hotel?

She was the bellhop.

What happened when two frogs tried to catch the same fly?

They ended up tongue-tied.

Giraffe

Giraffes are the highest form of life, and at school they have the highest marks.

Did you hear about the giraffe race?
It was neck-and-neck all the way.

Why are giraffes the snobbiest animals in the jungle?
Because they look down on everything.

A short poem on a tall subject:

Just think how long a tall giraffe
Would take to have a belly laugh.

Be like a giraffe. Reach higher than all the others, and you'll have the best view of life. You'll be head and shoulders above the rest of the herd, and everybody will look up to you.

Gnu

One day I went to the zoo,
For I wanted to see the old gnu.
But the old gnu was dead,
And the new gnu, they said,
Surely knew as a gnu he was new.

What do antelopes read every morning at breakfast?
The daily gnuspaper.

There once was a gnu in a zoo
That tired of the same daily view.
To seek a new site,
He stole out one night,
But where he went gnobody gnu.

Two lions were the leaders of their pride. While searching for their dinner, they came upon two unsuspecting gnus and ate them. "That," announced one of the kings of the jungle, "is the end of the gnus. And here, once again, are the head lions."

Or, as one antelope said to another on January 1, "Happy Gnu Deer!"

Goat

Goats have bad manners. They are always butting in.

Who babysits for the kids?
A nanny goat.

Why did the goat eat some fluorescent tubes?
He wanted a light lunch.

Did you hear about the angry farmer?
Someone got his goat.

What is the world's best butter?
A goat.

Goldfish

Mother: "Have you given the goldfish fresh water today?"

Son: "They haven't finished drinking what I gave them yesterday."

Why does a goldfish travel more than any other fish?
Because it swims around the globe.

As one goldfish said to another while swimming in a bowl, "See you around."

Goose

Two geese were watching the formation of Navy jets flying overhead, when one said, "I admit they're pretty clever flying without flapping their wings. But they needn't roar about it."

One goose turned to another at the back of a large "V" formation and asked, "Why do we always have to follow the same leader?"

Replied the other goose, "Because he's the one with the map."

As the baby goose said when it heard a car honk in the night, "Is that you, Mama?"

Gorilla

What do you call an 800-pound gorilla?
    Sir.

Where does an 800-pound gorilla sit?
        Anywhere she wants to.

What do you call chest-thumping and limb-swinging?
        Gorilla tactics.

41

Why do gorillas have big nostrils?
They have big fingers.

Knock, knock.
Who's there?
Gorilla.
Gorilla who?
Gorilla cheese sandwich for me, please.

Great Dane

Man: "Doctor, my Great Dane does nothing but chase sports cars."

Vet: "That's only natural. Most dogs chase cars."

Man: "Yes, but mine catches them and buries them in the backyard."

Did you hear about the Great Dane who was bought by an unsuspecting family?

He had the house broken before he was.

Hare

Rabbit fur is hare hair.

Did you hear about the rich rabbit?

He was a million-hare.

What do you call a clothing store for rabbits?

A hare dresser.

43

How do you recognize old rabbits?
By the gray hares.

A happily hopping hare suddenly collapsed in front of a barbershop. The barber grabbed one of his cans of spray and emptied it on the furry little animal. The hare rapidly recovered and, showing its gratitude, gestured with its paw as it hopped away.

This shows that the can has the right directions to deal with the problem: "Hair spray. Restores life in dead hair. Adds permanent wave."

Hawk

What kind of hawk has no wings?
A tomahawk.

Hen

Why did the hen sit on an axe?
So she could hatchet.

"It is not in my nature to fiddle,
And thumbs I am lacking to twiddle,"
Said the hen as with pride,
She laid sunny-side
Two fried eggs on a piping hot griddle.

What is a hen's favorite dessert?
Layer cake.

Why does a hen lay eggs?
Because if she dropped them, they would break.

What happens to hens that don't produce enough eggs?
They get laid off.

The codfish lays 10,000 eggs,
The lonely hen lays one.
The codfish never cackles
To tell you what she's done.

And so we scorn the codfish,
While the humble hen we prize,
Which only goes to show you
That it pays to advertise.

Herring

Did you hear about the partially deaf fish?
She was hard of herring.

Hippopotamus

Teacher: "What would Thanksgiving dinner be like if the Pilgrims had landed in Africa instead of America?"

Student: "I don't know, but I'd sure hate to try to stuff a hippopotamus."

As the large river beasts shouted when their team won a football game, "Hippo, hippo, hooray!"

There once was a jolly fat hippo
That jumped in the sea for a dippo.
It would have been wise
Had he opened his eyes,
But he didn't and flattened a ship, oh!

What animal is always laughing?
A happy-potamus.

Why couldn't Noah play cards in the ark?
Because a hippo was standing on the deck.

Hog

Did you hear about the pigs at a party?
They went whole hog and hog wild.

If you make hamburgers from ground beef, what do you make pork burgers from?
Ground hogs.

Horse

The beginner asked the instructor, "What's the hardest thing about learning to ride a horse?"
The instructor replied, "The ground."

How do you make a slow horse fast?
Don't feed it anything.

Why is a leaking faucet like a racehorse?
Because it's off and running.

Why are clouds like jockeys?
Because they hold the rains.

What is a horse's favorite sport?
Stable tennis.

Be like a horse. Use some horse sense and stable thinking and be able to say "nay."

Hyena

Why did the man cross a parrot and a hyena?
> *So he could ask it what it was laughing about.*

Knock, knock.
Who's there?
Hyena.
Hyena who?
Hyena tree sat a vulture.

Iguana

Tourist: "Do you have any lizards on this island?"
Native: "Iguana show you one."

Inchworm

How many night crawlers are there in a foot?
Twelve inchworms.

Insect

Patient: "Doctor, doctor! What's the best way to prevent diseases caused by biting insects?"

Doctor: "Don't bite any."

A couple spread their blanket in the woods, when the lady said, "What a lovely place for a picnic."

"It must be," replied the man. "Ten million insects can't be wrong."

Jackal

An unfunny beast is the jackal,
Which seems, indeed, to lack all
Sense of humor.
Well, that's the rumor,
For it's never been known to cackle.

How do wild dogs in the jungle see at night?
They use jackal lanterns.

Jellyfish

What does a jellyfish have on its tummy?

A jelly button.

What do jellyfish put their hotdogs in?

Jelly rolls.

What is a harbor policeman's favorite snack?

A peanut butter and jellyfish sandwich and a jellyfish donut.

Kangaroo

A kangaroo is a pogo stick with a pouch.

What is a kangaroo's favorite season?
Spring, especially in a leap year.

What is a kangaroo's favorite game?
Hopscotch.

Why do mother kangaroos hate it when it rains?
They don't like it when the children have to stay inside.

Did you hear about the kangaroos that got married?
They lived hoppily ever after.

What sounds do kangaroo Rice Krispies make?
Snap, crackle, and hop.

> *When a sailor in Santa Fe's zoo*
> *Snatched a cute little baby kangaroo,*
> *Its mother said, "Jack,*
> *You can put it right back.*
> *You know picking my pocket's taboo."*

Be like a kangaroo. Advance through life by leaps and bounds, and keep your family close to you.

Kitten

What do kitten announcers say on the radio?
Wee paws for station identification.

Why did the cat join the Red Cross?
She wanted to be a first aid kit.

Lemming

What advice did the mother lemming give to her son?

"Just because Johnny is jumping off a cliff doesn't mean you have to."

Why was the lemming so hesitant?

He didn't want to jump to a conclusion.

Leopard

What happened to the leopard that took a bath three times a day?

After a week, he was spotless.

A leopard went to see an eye doctor because he thought he needed an eye exam. "Every time I look at my wife," he worriedly told the optometrist, "I see spots before my eyes."

"So what's to worry about?" replied the doctor. "You're a leopard, aren't you?"

"What's that got to do with anything?" replied the patient. "My wife is a zebra."

> *There once was a handsome, young shepherd,*
> *Who was eaten at lunch by a leopard.*
> > *Said the leopard, "Egad!*
> > *You'd be tastier, lad,*
> *If you had been salted and peppered."*

Lion

Did you hear about the lion tamer who stuck his right arm in a lion's mouth?

> *They call him Lefty.*

Then there was the circus stuntman who used to stick both his left arm and left leg in a lion's mouth. He's all right now.

Did you hear about the new book titled *Lion Taming*?

> *It's by Claude Bottom.*

How does a lion greet the other animals in the wild?

> *"Pleased to eat you."*

What happened to the man who tried to cross a lion with a goat?

> *He had to get a new goat.*

As the lion said to the minister, "Let us prey."

Knock, knock.
Who's there?
Lion.
Lion who?
Lion to your parents will get you in trouble.

Lizard

What has a long tongue and walks on a yellow brick road?
> *The Lizard of Oz.*

What's the difference between a jumping magician and a crying gecko?
> *One is a leaping wizard, and the other is a weeping lizard.*

Llama

What do South American animals use to help them wake up?
> *A llama clock.*

Knock, knock.
Who's there?
Llama.
Llama who?
Llama Yankee Doodle Dandy.

Lobster

What lobster visits you on Christmas Eve?
> *Santa Claws.*

What did the lobster say when placed in a boiling pot?
> *"Am I in hot water!"*

Mare

Did you hear about the horse that kept late hours?
It was a nightmare.

Mockingbird

What happened to the mockingbird that swallowed a watch?
She became a tick-tocking bird.

Mole

Why are moles such uninteresting company?
Because they're always boring.

Why did the mole build a new house?
He was fed up with the hole thing.

Have you ever met a mole with a woman on its cheek?

Be like a mole. Stay down-to-earth and well-grounded. Move ahead by digging as deep as you can.

Monkey

Why did the chimpanzee like potato chips?
She was a chipmonkey.

What is a monkey's favorite fruit-flavored drink?
Oranga-Tang.

What do monkeys sing at Christmas?
"Jungle Bells, Jungle Bells."

What were King Kong's last words?
"Don't monkey around with me."

How did the monkey go from the second floor to the first floor?
She slid down the banana-ster.

Moose

What has antlers and eats cheese?
Mickey Moose.

What do moose do at a concert?
They make moosic.

How can you distinguish a male elk from a female?
> *By his moosetache.*

Mosquito

A mosquito is an insect that bites the hand that feeds it.

What makes mosquitoes annoying?
> *They get under your skin.*

Why was the mosquito limping?
> *He went in through a screen door and strained himself.*

Moth

Who spends the summer in a fur coat and the winter in a woolen bathing suit?
> *A moth.*

Mouse

What has six eyes but can't see?
> *Three blind mice.*

What is a cat's favorite foods?
> *Mice Krispies, Minute Mice, and Mice Cream.*

A mouse in her room woke Miss Dowd,
She was frightened, almost screamed aloud;
> *But a happy thought hit her:*
> *To scare off the critter,*
She sat up in bed and meowed.

Why is an old loaf of bread like a mouse dashing into its hole?

> *Because you can see it's stale.*

What do cats like on their hot dogs?
> *Catsup and mousetard.*

What has gray skin, four legs, and a trunk?
> *No, not an elephant—but a mouse on vacation.*

What is the favorite game of mice?
> *Hide and squeak.*

> *Hickory, dickory, dock,*
> *Some mice ran up the clock.*
> *The clock struck one,*
> *And the rest escaped with minor injuries.*

Mule

A mule is a stubborn animal that is backward about going forward.

Did you hear the joke about the mule?
> *You'll get a real kick out of it.*

Mussel

> *There once was a strong man named Russell,*
> *Who liked getting into a tussle.*
> > *But he once lost face*
> > *At a seafood place,*
> *When he struggled to open a mussel.*

Newt

What is a salamander's favorite treat?
  Fig Newt-ons.

What do salamanders like to watch on TV at night?
  The evening newts.

The salamander was actually a midget lizard, but no one newt.

Nightingale

What weather do nightingales hate the most?
  Spending the night in gales.

Octopus

What kind of cat likes water?

An octo-puss

What is an octopus's favorite song?

"I want to hold your hand, your hand, your hand . . . ."

Did you hear about the two octopuses that fell in love?

They walked arm in arm in arm in arm . . . .

Did you hear about the clever saleswoman?

She sold a supply of underarm deodorant to a family of octopuses.

Ostrich

An ostrich is the giraffe among birds.

Otter

What kind of vehicles do web-footed mammals drive?

Otter mobiles.

What is the Golden Rule for web-footed mammals?

"Do unto otters as you would have them do unto you."

Where do web-footed mammals live?

In otter space.

Said the otter to his daughter,
"Daughter, don't go near the water."
Said the daughter to her pater,
"I'm an otter, not a squatter."
Should he slap or maybe swat her?
Suppose a rotter otter spot her?
A slicker swain, a surly plotter,
A cad, a reputation-blotter?
The more he thought, he grew the hotter.
But all he said? "You shouldn't oughter."

Owl

Patient: "Doctor, doctor! I know a man who thinks he's an owl."

Doctor: "Who?"

Patient: "Now I know TWO people."

Did you hear about the comedian owl?
He was a real hoot.

A wise old owl sat in an oak.
The more he saw the less he spoke.
The less he spoke the more he heard.
Why can't we be like that wise old bird?

As the father owl said to his son, "It's not what you know, but whooo you know."

As the sea captain announced to his bird passenger, "Owl aboard!"

Be like an owl. Look all around, be wise, and give a hoot.

Oyster

A noise annoys an oyster.

Did you hear about the shy oyster?
It crawled into its shell and clammed up.

An oyster met an oyster, and they were oysters two;
Two oysters met two oysters, and they were oysters, too;
Four oysters met a cup of milk, and they were oyster stew.

There was a woman who was so polite that she wouldn't open an oyster without knocking on its shell first.

What is chocolate and lies on the bottom of the ocean?
An oyster egg.

Be like an oyster. It takes a lot of grit to make a pearl of great value.

Parrot

A parrot is a wordy birdy.

What's orange and sounds like a parrot?
A carrot.

What did the parrot say when it saw a duck?
"Polly wants a quacker."

What do you get when you cross a parrot with a lion?
*An animal that says, "Polly wants a cracker—
NOW!"*

Did you hear about the parrot that swallowed a watch?

Now it goes tick-talk-tick-talk.

What do you call birds that like to attack ships?

Parrots of the Caribbean.

Why did the talking bird join the Air Force?

He wanted to be a parrot-trooper.

Peacock

A peacock is a chicken in bloom, a Technicolor turkey.

Did you hear the story about the peacock?

It's a beautiful tale.

Why are peacocks unreliable?

They're always spreading tails.

Why is the figure "9" like a peacock?

Because without its tail, it's nothing.

Peacocks pay careful attention to de tail.

Pelican

Consider the fabulous pelican:
His mouth can hold more than his belican.
He can store in his beak
Enough food for a week.
And it's truly amazing how wellican!

What do you call a big-billed bird with a negative attitude?

A pelican't.

Why do pelicans carry fish in their beaks?

Because they don't have any pockets.

Penguin

What's black and white and has eight wheels?

A penguin on roller skates.

What is a penguin's favorite vehicle?

An ice-cycle.

What do penguins wear to keep their heads warm?

Polar ice caps.

Did you hear about the guy who used a computer dating service and requested someone who was short, liked water sports, and wore formal attire?

The computer set him up with a penguin.

Pet

Sign in a veterinarian's waiting room: Back in 10 Minutes. Sit! Stay!

Pig

Where do hogs keep their money?

In piggy banks.

One pig said to another on a very hot day, "I never sausage heat."

The other pig replied, "Yeah, and I'm almost bacon."

What do you call someone who steals pigs?

A hamburglar.

What's the best move by a pig that knows karate?

A pork chop.

Pigeon

What happened when the pigeon swooped down?

The dove dove.

Did you hear about the girl who is like a dove?

She's not soft and cooing, but she is pigeon-toed.

Polar Bear

What is an Arctic bear's favorite sport?

Polar vaulting.

What is a polar bear's favorite food?

Icebergers.

Polliwog

A parrot that lived near a bog
Met a prince in the form of a frog.
Now she and her prince
Are the parents of quints:
Four girls and one polly-wog.

Pony

A pony with a sore throat is a hoarse horse.

How is a drama teacher like the Pony Express?
> *He's a stage coach.*

Poodle

How can you tell if it's raining cats and dogs?
> *When you step in a poodle.*

Why did the man describe his dog as a miniature poodle?
> *Because the miniature back is turned, it makes a poodle.*

Did you hear about the dog that enjoys having his hair washed every day?
> *He's a shampoodle.*

> *There once was a man with two poodles*
> *Whose first names were Doodles and Toodles.*
> > *Their favorite dish*
> > *Was not meat or fish.*
> *The poodles loved oodles of noodles.*

Porcupine

How do porcupines kiss?
> *Very carefully.*

As the father porcupine said to his son as he was about to spank him, "This is going to hurt me more than it's going to hurt you."

What pine has the sharpest needles?
Porcupines.

As the baby porcupine said when it bumped into a cactus plant during the night, "Is that you, Mama?"

What did the porcupine couple name their son?
Spike.

What's worse than a rhinoceros on water skis?
A porcupine on a rubber raft.

Porpoise

As one dolphin said, after accidentally swimming into another one, "I didn't do it on porpoise."

Puffin

Did you hear about the bird that was out of shape?
She was a huffin' puffin.

Puma

A jolly young fellow from Yuma
Told an elephant joke to a puma.
Now his skeleton lies
Under hot western skies.
The puma had no sense of huma.

Puppy

A puppy is a little waggin' without wheels.

Where do baby dogs sleep on camping trips?
In pup tents.

Quahog

Did you hear about the animal that was crazy about clams?

He went quahog wild.

Quail

Who's boss between a father and mother quail?
Neither. They're e-quail.

What did the game birds sing at a family reunion?
"Quail, quail, the gang's all here."

Rabbit

What did Bugs Bunny says to the pier?
"What's up, dock?"

Where do newly married rabbits go?
On their bunnymoon.

> *The habits of rabbits*
> *Are such, it's agreed,*
> *That dozens of cousins*
> *Are common indeed.*

What did the bunny say to the clerk after she bought a holiday gift?

"Rabbit up."

What's invisible and smells like carrots?

Bunny breath.

Teacher: "If I give you two rabbits and two more rabbits and then another two, how many rabbits will you have?"

Student: "Seven."

Teacher: "Are you sure that the answer isn't six?"

Student: "It's seven. I already have a rabbit at home."

What's a rabbit's favorite dance style?

Hip-hop.

Rattlesnake

How do you make a baby or a snake cry?

Take away its rattle.

A rattlesnake has a tattle tail.

Reindeer

Why did Santa use only seven reindeer last year?

Comet stayed home to clean the sink.

Wife: "How is a cloud like Santa Claus?"

Husband: "It holds rain, dear."

Among the reindeer that pull Santa Claus's sleigh, you surely know about Olive, the other reindeer.

Rhinoceros

Be like a rhino. Be thick-skinned and charge ahead to make your point.

Robin

A robin is a sparrow that spilled ketchup on its chest.

Did you hear about the criminal bird?
He was always robin banks.

Why was Batman so depressed?
Because Robin flew south for the winter.

Rooster

What does a lazy rooster say?
"Cock-a-doodle-don't."

Why did the rooster cross the road?
The hen egged him on.

Salmon

What is a young fish's favorite game?
Salmon says.

Sardine

What happened to the sardine factory employees who
didn't show up for work?
They got canned.

The survivor of a shipwreck told reporters, "I had to live
for a week on a can of sardines."

A voice in the back asked, "Weren't you afraid of falling
off?"

Seagull

Where do seagulls go to the movies?
The dive-in.

What do you call a man with a seagull on his head?
Cliff.

What bird enjoys soccer?
A gull keeper.

Signs on a seafood restaurant's restrooms: "Buoys" and "Gulls."

Two men were walking along the beach when a seagull plunked a load right smack in one guy's eye.
The other fellow thoughtfully offered, "Let me get some toilet paper."
"Forget it," the victim replied. "It's probably a mile away by now."

Seahorse

Why did the sportsman buy a seahorse?
He wanted to play water polo.

Seal

What is a seal's favorite subject in school?
ART-ART-ART.

Did you hear about the guy who went on a raw fish diet?
He didn't lose much weight, but he can balance a ball on his nose and bark like a seal.

Seeing-Eye Dog

Did you hear about the two seeing-eye dogs who went on a blind date?

Why don't blind people like to skydive?
Because it scares the heck out of the dog.

Shark

What happened when a shark tried to eat a crate of gum?
He bit off more than he could chew.

Man No. 1: "I saw a man-eating shark at the aquarium."
Man No. 2: "Big deal. I saw a man eating mahi-mahi in a restaurant."

What is a shark's favorite game?
Swallow the Feeder.

Sheep

Dogs have fleas, and sheep have fleece.

Did you hear the song about a lamb that has just been sheared?
"Bare, bare, back sheep."

A tourist asked a farmer how many sheep he had. "I don't know," was the reply. "Every time I try to count them, I fall asleep."

Did you hear about Shep Sheep, the comedian?
He was a master of baaad jokes, and he had three bags full of them. His sign-off line was, "If I don't see you in the future, I'll see you in the pasture."

When they are trying to fall asleep, do sheep count people?

How many sheep does it take to make a sweater?
It depends on how well they can knit.

Sheepdog

What animal goes, "Baaa! Woof! Baaa! Arf!"?
A sheepdog.

Skunk

A skunk is a community scenter.

How do you stop a skunk from smelling?
Hold its nose.

There was a young man from the city
Who met what he thought was a kitty.
He gave it a pat
And said, "Nice little cat."
They buried his clothes out of pity.

What did one skunk say to another when they were cornered outside a church?
"Let us spray."

Are skunks good at games?
No, they stink at everything.

What's a skunk's favorite game in school?
Show-and-smell.

Why are skunks so smart?
They have a lot of scents.

Snail

What is the strongest animal?
The snail, because it carries its house on its back.

Where do snails go to eat?
Slow-food restaurants.

As the snail said to the turtle, "What's the rush?"

What do snails use to paint their toes?

Snail polish.

A snail was slowly crawling up an apple tree during the winter. A squirrel spied the snail and said, "You're wasting your time. There aren't any apples up there."

The snail replied, "There will be when I get there."

Snake

Boy No. 1: "I saw a six-foot snake."

Boy No. 2: "I didn't think snakes had feet."

What is a snake's favorite vegetable?

Coily-flower.

Did you hear about the nearsighted snake that finally was fitted with glasses?

> *He discovered that his wife was actually a garden hose.*

Why don't snakes do well at school?

> *Because they can't raise their hands to answer the teacher's questions.*

What is a snake's favorite subject in school?

Hisstory.

Sow

How much money is the owner of 100 female pigs and 100 male deer worth?

Two hundred sows and bucks.

Spider

Why are spiders like toy tops?

Because they're always spinning.

Why was the spider late for her date?

It took her so long to put in eight contact lenses.

Why did the fly fly?

Because the spider spied her.

Why did the spider play baseball?

He liked catching flies.

What did Miss Muffet say when the spider asked her for a date?

"Ha! No whey!"

As one techie spider said to another, "Have you checked out my web site?"

Be like a spider. Surf the web and pull the right strings.

Sponge

What is full of holes but still holds water?

A sponge.

Here's an absorbing question: Would the ocean be higher if there weren't so many sponges in it?

Be like a sponge. Soak up everything, and be helpful in the kitchen.

Squirrel

Boy squirrel: "I'm just nuts about you."

Girl squirrel: "You're nut so bad yourself."

What do you call a crazy squirrel in a spaceship?

An astronut.

Be like a squirrel, bright-eyed and bushy-tailed. Go out on a limb to prepare for hard times.

Starfish

What kind of fish comes out at night?

Starfish.

Stork

A stork is a baby bird.

Who delivers baby whales?

A stork with a bad back.

Swallow

What bird is present at every meal?

A swallow.

Swordfish

What was the favorite food of King Arthur and his knights?

Swordfish.

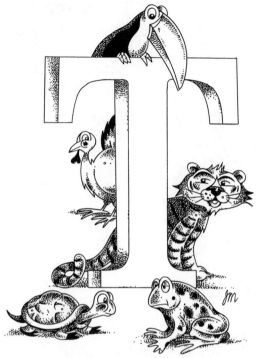

Tadpole

Did you hear about the frog that hung a flag on a tadpole?

Termite

Did you hear about the termites that invited themselves to dinner?

They ate a family out of house and home.

After two termites got married, they lived happily ever rafter.

What was the pirate's downfall?

An attack of termites on his wooden leg.

Tick

What kind of bugs live in clocks?
Ticks.

Tiger

Why do tigers have stripes?
So they won't be spotted.

Man No. 1: "Would you rather have a lion attack you or a tiger?"
Man No. 2: "I'd rather it attacked the tiger."

What are the most popular flowers in a zoo?
The dandelion and the tiger lily.

What is a tiger's favorite book?
Revenge of the Tiger, by Claude Arms.

> *There was a young lady from Niger*
> *Who smiled as she rode on a tiger.*
> *They returned from the ride*
> *With the lady inside,*
> *And a smile on the face of the tiger.*

Toad

What do you call a dragged cousin of a frog?
A towed toad.

How do amphibians get to the Land of Oz?
They follow the yellow brick toad.

What happened to the illegally parked amphibians?
They got toad away.

What kind of shoes do frogs wear?
Open-toad sandals.

Or, as the frustrated father frog said to his daughter, "If I've toad you once, I've toad you a thousand times . . ."

Tuna

Did you hear about the fish that knows notes in all scales?

It was a piano tuna.

Why do some men prefer to go fishing alone?

Because they think tuna boat is one too many.

Turkey

Why did they let the turkey join the band?

Because it had the drumsticks.

Is turkey soup good for your health?

Not if you're the turkey.

Why did the turkey cross the road?

To show he wasn't chicken.

Which side of the turkey has the most feathers?

The outside.

Why did the turkey bolt down his food?

Because he was a gobbler.

Why do turkeys have such difficult lives?

Because they're cut to pieces, they have the stuffing knocked out of them, and they're picked on for days after Thanksgiving.

Turtle

A turtle is a reptile with a mobile home.

Did you hear about the nearsighted turtle?

He fell in love with an army helmet.

What do you call a tortoise that is an informer?

A turtle-tale.

Why did the turtle cross the road?

To get to the Shell station.

What is the favorite name for girl turtles?

Michelle.

How did the turtle pay for his meal?

By shelling out cash.

Be like a turtle. You'll make progress by coming out of your shell and sticking your neck out.

Unicorn

It is risky business to play leapfrog with a unicorn.

As one mythical creature said to another, "Unicorniest guy I ever met."

Vampire

Dracula can be a real pain in the neck, and he can get under your skin and drive you batty.

What do vampires take for a sore throat?

Coffin drops.

What is a vampire's favorite animal?

The giraffe. There's so much neck to gnaw on.

Why did the vampire go into a fast-food restaurant?
For a quick bite.

How many vampires does it take to change a light bulb?
None. Vampires prefer the dark.

Knock, knock.
Who's there?
Ivan.
Ivan who?
Ivan to drink your blood.

How do you say good-bye to a vampire?
"So long, sucker!"

Vulture

What is a vulture's favorite meal?
Leftovers.

What is a vulture's favorite game?
Scavenger hunts.

What did one vulture say to another?
"I've got a bone to pick with you."

What kind of luggage do vultures take on airplanes?
Carrion.

Wallaby

As one kangaroo said to another, "Wallaby a monkey's uncle!"

Wasp

Where do sick hornets go?
To the waspital.

Weasel

What is the favorite song of certain small, long-tailed mammals?
"Weasel While You Work."

Weevil

What kind of insects are found in tenpins alleys?
Bowl weevils.

Werewolf

Where does a werewolf live?
In a werehouse.

What do you get when you cross a werewolf with a clay spinner?
A hairy potter.

A man visited his doctor and complained, "Doctor, doctor! I feel that I'm turning into a werewolf!"
The doctor replied, "Relax. Have a seat and comb your face."

Whale

What do whales chew?
Blubber gum.

Do whales ever cry?
Yes. Haven't you ever seen whales blubber?

Did you hear about the gossipy whale?
It was a blubber mouth.

What's the favorite game show of large mammals?
Whale of Fortune.

Wolf

Why are wolves like playing cards?
Because they belong to a pack.

Did you hear about the wolf comedian?
He had his audience howling with laughter.

Where do wolf movie stars live?
In Howlywood.

Where do wolves stay on vacation?
At the Howliday Inn.

Woodchuck

*How much wood would a woodchuck chuck
If a woodchuck could chuck wood?
A woodchuck would chuck
All the wood that a woodchuck could chuck
If a woodchuck would chuck wood.*

Woodpecker

What is green and pecks on trees?
Woody Woodpickle.

A woodpecker in the woods took a powerful peck at the trunk of a huge oak tree, and at the very same instant a bolt of lightning struck and felled the tree. The amazed woodpecker said to himself, "Wow! I didn't realize my own strength!"

Why did the homeowner get mad at the woodpecker?
He was sick and tired of saying, "Come in."

Be like the woodpecker. Just keep pecking away until you finish the job. You'll succeed by using your head and proving that opportunity knocks more than once.

Worm

Ooey Gooey was a worm,
A wondrous worm was he.
He stepped upon a railroad track;
A train he did not see.
Ooey Gooey.

Did you hear about the two silkworms that were in a race?
Neither won because they ended up in a tie.

Did all the animals enter Noah's ark in pairs?
No. The worms came in apples.

Why couldn't Noah catch many fish?
He had only two worms.

Two worms met coming out of their holes in the ground.
"I think I'm in love with you," gushed the first.
"Don't be ridiculous," replied the second. "I'm your other end."

What happened to the worm in a cornfield?
It went in one ear and out the other.

What's worse than biting into an apple and finding a worm?
Finding half a worm.

Wren

Why are boys and girls like a shivering bird?
*Boys and girls are children, and a shivering bird is
a chilled wren.*

*There was an old man quite un-sheared,
Who said, "It is just as I feared:
     Three hawks and a hen,
     Four rooks and a wren
Have all built their nests in my beard."*

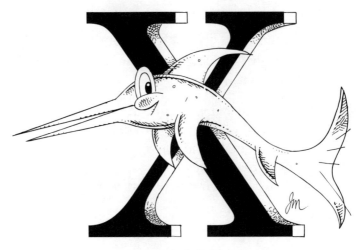

Xiphiidae

There's a little-known animal that begins with the letter **X**. It's actually a Greek swordfish, spelled x-i-p-h-i-i-d-a-e, and it's pronounced "ziff-EYE-ih-dee." With that in mind, let's take an alphabetical safari of animals A-Z.

Aardvark a million miles to put 26 animal puns in alphabetical order. I'd **badger** you, and I'd keep **carp**ing on the subject, until I had no **ideers** left. I'd have no **egrets**, however, as I **ferret**ed out more animal puns. If necessary, I'd even **gopher** broke. Some may say it would be a **hare**-brained attempt, but, **iguana** tell you, I'm no **jackass**—and I **kid** you not. I'm not doing this for a **lark** (although maybe just a **mite**). So don't **nag** me. In fact, you **otter** try to **parrot** me. But don't **quail** from the challenge. No one will accuse you of **robin** a bank. Don't be **shellfish**. Avoid taking a **tern** for the worse. Don't be afraid of people saying to you, "**unicorn**iest person I know." Stop crying and **viper** nose. Then say, "**wallaby** a son-of-a-gun" and start singing, "Zip-a-dee doo-dah, **xiphiidae**-ay." Soon you'll be a **yak**-of-all-trades, and can put all of these animal puns in a book called *Who's Zoo!*

Yak

Did you hear about the talkative Tibetan ox?
He was a yackety-yak.

What's the favorite children's toy in Tibet?
A yak-in-the-box.

What is the favorite children's story in Tibet?
"Yak the Giant Killer."

Who was the infamous Tibetan vampire?
Count Yakula.

> *There once was a man in Tibet*
> *Who worked in the hills as a vet.*
> *He treated the backs*
> *Of overworked yaks.*
> *How low (or how high) can one get?*

Zebra

If the alphabet goes from A to Z, then what goes from Z to A?

Zebra.

Did you hear about the zebra that fell in love with a horse that had sat down on a freshly painted park bench?

Did you hear about the zebra in a hurricane?

He had to glue on his stripes.

What has stars and stripes?

A movie about a zebra.

Did you hear about the nearsighted guy who bought a pet zebra?

He named it Spot.